This is _____
Verse Mapping
Bible Study Journal

Verse Mapping Bible Study Journal
Copyright © (2021) by Vanessa Tolic, All Rights Reserved

Cover Design by Vanessa Tolic

Introduction and Guide to Verse Mapping

What is Bible Verse Mapping?
Verse mapping is a method of studying the historical context, translation, connotation, and theological framework of a verse in the Bible. In short, verse mapping is a tool used to understand the deeper meaning of a verse.

The goal of this journal is to provide a structured approach to studying the Bible and its versus in context. Throughout the mapping process the aim is to:

- understand the meaning of the verse in its original language,
- identifying keywords and what those keywords actually mean,
- what the passage might have meant to the original audience,
- what it means to you today,
- and how can you use your new found knowledge in the future.

Verse mapping provides a structured approach to analyze different words, themes, and the history behind each verse that you are studying.

If this sounds overwhelming, with the right tools it can be made quite simple. You only need 5 things:
- a Bible,
- a concordance (Biblehub.com is a great reference tool),
- a language tool (again Biblehub.com has you covered),
- this journal,
- your favorite pens and highlighters

The six steps to Verse Mapping
By following the six simple steps below you can be mining the Bible which will help you to not only understand the Bible better, but also perhaps understand yourself better.

Step 1. Select a verse to study, this could be:
- your favorite verse,
- a verse your simply curious about
- a verse containing a topic you're interesting in
- a verse you're currently studying elsewhere.

Step 2. Search and discover the different translations of the verse.
Reading a verse in a different translation can provide you with a new insight into the verse as many words in Hebrew or Greek can be translated in different way to English.

Step 3. Highlight and circle keywords
Identify the key phrases or repeated words and look up the Hebrew or Greek meaning. It is important to remember that a word used in the Bible may have had a different meaning and connotation thousands of years ago in its original language.

Step 4. Context of the verse
Now that you have a better understanding of what is being said in its original language/s it is time to explore the context of the verse.
We can do this by asking questions about the verse, such as:
- what is happening immediately before and after this verse?
- who is the audience & who is the verse about?
- what is the main subject and how would it have been interpreted?
- where was the written and where did the audience live?
- when was this written?

Step 5. Your Takeaway
This is where you note down what your overall interpretation of the verse is and what is means to you. Noteworthy points include:
- any further questions and answers you want to seek out
- a summary of what you have learnt from this verse
- what you want to remember from this verse

Step 6. Future Application
The last step involves taking your new found knowledge and applying that knowledge to your life moving forward. Do you need to make any changes in your life based on what you have learnt? Has the way you view a topic or situation changed? Are there any promises you can commit to based on what you have learnt? Once these questions have been answered it is a great time to prayer!

I hope you enjoy this journal and it gain some valuable insights from it.

- Vanessa Tolic

Contents

Page	Verse	Page	Verse
_____	_____	_____	_____
_____	_____	_____	_____
_____	_____	_____	_____
_____	_____	_____	_____
_____	_____	_____	_____
_____	_____	_____	_____
_____	_____	_____	_____
_____	_____	_____	_____
_____	_____	_____	_____
_____	_____	_____	_____
_____	_____	_____	_____
_____	_____	_____	_____
_____	_____	_____	_____
_____	_____	_____	_____
_____	_____	_____	_____
_____	_____	_____	_____
_____	_____	_____	_____
_____	_____	_____	_____
_____	_____	_____	_____
_____	_____	_____	_____

Contents

Page	Verse	Page	Verse
————	————————————	————	————————————
————	————————————	————	————————————
————	————————————	————	————————————
————	————————————	————	————————————
————	————————————	————	————————————
————	————————————	————	————————————
————	————————————	————	————————————
————	————————————	————	————————————
————	————————————	————	————————————
————	————————————	————	————————————
————	————————————	————	————————————
————	————————————	————	————————————
————	————————————	————	————————————
————	————————————	————	————————————
————	————————————	————	————————————
————	————————————	————	————————————
————	————————————	————	————————————
————	————————————	————	————————————
————	————————————	————	————————————

Contents

Page	Verse		Page	Verse
_____	_____		_____	_____
_____	_____		_____	_____
_____	_____		_____	_____
_____	_____		_____	_____
_____	_____		_____	_____
_____	_____		_____	_____
_____	_____		_____	_____
_____	_____		_____	_____
_____	_____		_____	_____
_____	_____		_____	_____
_____	_____		_____	_____
_____	_____		_____	_____
_____	_____		_____	_____
_____	_____		_____	_____
_____	_____		_____	_____
_____	_____		_____	_____
_____	_____		_____	_____
_____	_____		_____	_____
_____	_____		_____	_____

BIBLE VERSE MAPPING

1 *The Verse*

Date : ___/___/___

2 *Translations of the verse*

3 *Keywords and definitions*

4 *Context of Verse*

Surrounding verses :

Who :

What :

Where :

When :

5 *Main Takeaway*

6 *Future Application*

BIBLE VERSE MAPPING

1 *The Verse*

2 *Translations of the verse*

3 *Keywords and definitions*

4 *Context of Verse*

Surrounding verses :

Who :

What :

Where :

When :

5 *Main Takeaway*

6 *Future Application*

BIBLE VERSE MAPPING

1 *The Verse*

Date : ___ / ___ / ___

2 *Translations of the verse*

3 *Keywords and definitions*

4 *Context of Verse*

Surrounding verses :

Who :

What :

Where :

When :

5 *Main Takeaway*

6 *Future Application*

BIBLE VERSE MAPPING

1 *The Verse*

Date : ____/ ____/ ____

2 *Translations of the verse*

3 *Keywords and definitions*

4 *Context of Verse*

Surrounding verses :

Who :   What :

Where :   When :

5 *Main Takeaway*

6 *Future Application*

BIBLE VERSE MAPPING

1 *The Verse*

Date : ___/___/___

2 *Translations of the verse*

3 *Keywords and definitions*

4 *Context of Verse*

Surrounding verses :

Who :

What :

Where :

When :

5 *Main Takeaway*

6 *Future Application*

BIBLE VERSE MAPPING

1 *The Verse*

Date : ___/___/___

2 *Translations of the verse*

3 *Keywords and definitions*

4 *Context of Verse*

Surrounding verses :

Who :

What :

Where :

When :

5 *Main Takeaway*

6 *Future Application*

BIBLE VERSE MAPPING

1 *The Verse*

Date : ___/ ___/ ___

2 *Translations of the verse*

3 *Keywords and definitions*

4 *Context of Verse*

Surrounding verses :

Who :

What :

Where :

When :

5 *Main Takeaway*

6 *Future Application*

BIBLE VERSE MAPPING

1 *The Verse*

Date : ___/ ___/ ___

2 *Translations of the verse*

3 *Keywords and definitions*

4 *Context of Verse*

Surrounding verses :

Who :

What :

Where :

When :

5 *Main Takeaway*

6 *Future Application*

BIBLE VERSE MAPPING

1 *The Verse*

Date : ___/ ___/ ___

2 *Translations of the verse*

3 *Keywords and definitions*

4 *Context of Verse*

Surrounding verses :

Who :

What :

Where :

When :

5 *Main Takeaway*

6 *Future Application*

BIBLE VERSE MAPPING

1 *The Verse*

Date : ___ / ___ / ___

2 *Translations of the verse*

3 *Keywords and definitions*

4 *Context of Verse*

Surrounding verses :

Who :

What :

Where :

When :

5 *Main Takeaway*

6 *Future Application*

BIBLE VERSE MAPPING

1 The Verse

Date : ____ / ____ / ____

2 Translations of the verse

3 Keywords and definitions

4 Context of Verse

Surrounding verses :

Who :

What :

Where :

When :

5 Main Takeaway

6 Future Application

BIBLE VERSE MAPPING

1 The Verse

2 Translations of the verse

3 Keywords and definitions

4 Context of Verse

Surrounding verses :

Who :   What :

Where :   When :

5 Main Takeaway

6 Future Application

BIBLE VERSE MAPPING

1 The Verse

Date : ___/___/___

2 Translations of the verse

3 Keywords and definitions

4 Context of Verse

Surrounding verses :

Who :

What :

Where :

When :

5 Main Takeaway

6 Future Application

BIBLE VERSE MAPPING

1 *The Verse*

Date : ___/ ___/ ___

2 *Translations of the verse*

3 *Keywords and definitions*

4 *Context of Verse*

Surrounding verses :

Who :   What :

Where :   When :

5 *Main Takeaway*

6 *Future Application*

BIBLE VERSE MAPPING

1 *The Verse*

Date : ___/___/___

2 *Translations of the verse*

3 *Keywords and definitions*

4 *Context of Verse*

Surrounding verses :

Who :

What :

Where :

When :

5 *Main Takeaway*

6 *Future Application*

BIBLE VERSE MAPPING

1 *The Verse*

Date : ___ / ___ / ___

2 *Translations of the verse*

3 *Keywords and definitions*

4 *Context of Verse*

Surrounding verses :

Who :

What :

Where :

When :

5 *Main Takeaway*

6 *Future Application*

BIBLE VERSE MAPPING

1 *The Verse*

Date : ____/ ____/ ____

2 *Translations of the verse*

3 *Keywords and definitions*

4 *Context of Verse*

Surrounding verses :

Who :

What :

Where :

When :

5 *Main Takeaway*

6 *Future Application*

BIBLE VERSE MAPPING

1 *The Verse*

Date : ___/___/___

2 *Translations of the verse*

3 *Keywords and definitions*

4 *Context of Verse*

Surrounding verses :

Who :

What :

Where :

When :

5 *Main Takeaway*

6 *Future Application*

BIBLE VERSE MAPPING

1 *The Verse*

Date : ___ / ___ / ___

2 *Translations of the verse*

3 *Keywords and definitions*

4 *Context of Verse*

Surrounding verses :

Who :

What :

Where :

When :

5 *Main Takeaway*

6 *Future Application*

BIBLE VERSE MAPPING

1 *The Verse*

Date : ___ / ___ / ___

2 *Translations of the verse*

3 *Keywords and definitions*

4 *Context of Verse*

Surrounding verses :

Who :

What :

Where :

When :

5 *Main Takeaway*

6 *Future Application*

BIBLE VERSE MAPPING

1 The Verse

Date : ___ / ___ / ___

2 Translations of the verse

3 Keywords and definitions

4 Context of Verse

Surrounding verses :

Who :

What :

Where :

When :

5 Main Takeaway

6 Future Application

BIBLE VERSE MAPPING

1 *The Verse*

Date : ___ / ___ / ___

2 *Translations of the verse*

3 *Keywords and definitions*

4 *Context of Verse*

Surrounding verses :

Who :

What :

Where :

When :

5 *Main Takeaway*

6 *Future Application*

BIBLE VERSE MAPPING

1 *The Verse*

Date : ___ / ___ / ___

2 *Translations of the verse*

3 *Keywords and definitions*

4 *Context of Verse*

Surrounding verses :

Who :

What :

Where :

When :

5 *Main Takeaway*

6 *Future Application*

BIBLE VERSE MAPPING

1 *The Verse*

2 *Translations of the verse*

3 *Keywords and definitions*

4 *Context of Verse*

Surrounding verses :

Who :

What :

Where :

When :

5 *Main Takeaway*

6 *Future Application*

BIBLE VERSE MAPPING

1 *The Verse*

Date : ___/___/___

2 *Translations of the verse*

3 *Keywords and definitions*

4 *Context of Verse*

Surrounding verses :

Who :   What :

Where :   When :

5 *Main Takeaway*

6 *Future Application*

BIBLE VERSE MAPPING

1 The Verse

Date : ___/___/___

2 Translations of the verse

3 Keywords and definitions

4 Context of Verse

Surrounding verses :

Who :   What :

Where :   When :

5 Main Takeaway

6 Future Application

BIBLE VERSE MAPPING

1 *The Verse*

Date : ___/___/___

2 *Translations of the verse*

3 *Keywords and definitions*

4 *Context of Verse*

Surrounding verses :

Who :

What :

Where :

When :

5 *Main Takeaway*

6 *Future Application*

BIBLE VERSE MAPPING

1 *The Verse*

Date : ___/___/___

2 *Translations of the verse*

3 *Keywords and definitions*

4 *Context of Verse*

Surrounding verses :

Who :

What :

Where :

When :

5 *Main Takeaway*

6 *Future Application*

BIBLE VERSE MAPPING

1 *The Verse*

2 *Translations of the verse*

3 *Keywords and definitions*

4 *Context of Verse*

Surrounding verses :

Who :

What :

Where :

When :

5 *Main Takeaway*

6 *Future Application*

BIBLE VERSE MAPPING

1 *The Verse*

Date : ___ / ___ / ___

2 *Translations of the verse*

3 *Keywords and definitions*

4 *Context of Verse*

Surrounding verses :

Who :

What :

Where :

When :

5 *Main Takeaway*

6 *Future Application*

BIBLE VERSE MAPPING

1 *The Verse*

Date : ___ / ___ / ___

2 *Translations of the verse*

3 *Keywords and definitions*

4 *Context of Verse*

Surrounding verses :

Who :

What :

Where :

When :

5 *Main Takeaway*

6 *Future Application*

BIBLE VERSE MAPPING

1 *The Verse*

Date : ___ / ___ / ___

2 *Translations of the verse*

3 *Keywords and definitions*

4 *Context of Verse*

Surrounding verses :

Who :

What :

Where :

When :

5 *Main Takeaway*

6 *Future Application*

BIBLE VERSE MAPPING

1 *The Verse*

Date : ___/___/___

2 *Translations of the verse*

3 *Keywords and definitions*

4 *Context of Verse*

Surrounding verses :

Who :   What :

Where :   When :

5 *Main Takeaway*

6 *Future Application*

BIBLE VERSE MAPPING

1 *The Verse*

2 *Translations of the verse*

3 *Keywords and definitions*

4 *Context of Verse*

Surrounding verses :

Who :

What :

Where :

When :

5 *Main Takeaway*

6 *Future Application*

BIBLE VERSE MAPPING

1 The Verse

Date : ___ / ___ / ___

2 Translations of the verse

3 Keywords and definitions

4 Context of Verse

Surrounding verses :

Who :

What :

Where :

When :

5 Main Takeaway

6 Future Application

BIBLE VERSE MAPPING

1 *The Verse*   *Date :* ___/___/___

2 *Translations of the verse*   **3** *Keywords and definitions*

4 *Context of Verse*

Surrounding verses :

Who :   *What :*

Where :   *When :*

5 *Main Takeaway*   **6** *Future Application*

BIBLE VERSE MAPPING

1 The Verse

Date : ___ / ___ / ___

2 Translations of the verse

3 Keywords and definitions

4 Context of Verse

Surrounding verses :

Who :

What :

Where :

When :

5 Main Takeaway

6 Future Application

BIBLE VERSE MAPPING

1 *The Verse*   *Date :* ___/___/___

2 *Translations of the verse*   **3** *Keywords and definitions*

4 *Context of Verse*

Surrounding verses :

Who :   *What :*

Where :   *When :*

5 *Main Takeaway*   **6** *Future Application*

BIBLE VERSE MAPPING

1 *The Verse*

Date : ___ / ___ / ___

2 *Translations of the verse*

3 *Keywords and definitions*

4 *Context of Verse*

Surrounding verses :

Who :

What :

Where :

When :

5 *Main Takeaway*

6 *Future Application*

BIBLE VERSE MAPPING

1 *The Verse*

Date : ___/___/___

2 *Translations of the verse*

3 *Keywords and definitions*

4 *Context of Verse*

Surrounding verses :

Who :   What :

Where :   When :

5 *Main Takeaway*

6 *Future Application*

BIBLE VERSE MAPPING

1 *The Verse*

Date : ___ / ___ / ___

2 *Translations of the verse*

3 *Keywords and definitions*

4 *Context of Verse*

Surrounding verses :

Who :

What :

Where :

When :

5 *Main Takeaway*

6 *Future Application*

BIBLE VERSE MAPPING

1 The Verse   Date : ___/___/___

2 Translations of the verse   **3** Keywords and definitions

4 Context of Verse

Surrounding verses :

Who :   What :

Where :   When :

5 Main Takeaway   **6** Future Application

BIBLE VERSE MAPPING

1 *The Verse*   *Date :* ___/___/___

2 *Translations of the verse*   **3** *Keywords and definitions*

4 *Context of Verse*

Surrounding verses :

Who :   What :

Where :   When :

5 *Main Takeaway*   **6** *Future Application*

BIBLE VERSE MAPPING

1 *The Verse*

2 *Translations of the verse*

3 *Keywords and definitions*

4 *Context of Verse*

Surrounding verses :

Who :

What :

Where :

When :

5 *Main Takeaway*

6 *Future Application*

BIBLE VERSE MAPPING

1 *The Verse*

Date : ___/___/___

2 *Translations of the verse*

3 *Keywords and definitions*

4 *Context of Verse*

Surrounding verses :

Who :   What :

Where :   When :

5 *Main Takeaway*

6 *Future Application*

BIBLE VERSE MAPPING

1 *The Verse*

2 *Translations of the verse*

3 *Keywords and definitions*

4 *Context of Verse*

Surrounding verses :

Who :   What :

Where :   When :

5 *Main Takeaway*

6 *Future Application*

BIBLE VERSE MAPPING

1 *The Verse*

Date : ___ / ___ / ___

2 *Translations of the verse*

3 *Keywords and definitions*

4 *Context of Verse*

Surrounding verses :

Who :

What :

Where :

When :

5 *Main Takeaway*

6 *Future Application*

BIBLE VERSE MAPPING

1 *The Verse*

2 *Translations of the verse*

3 *Keywords and definitions*

4 *Context of Verse*

Surrounding verses :

Who :   What :

Where :   When :

5 *Main Takeaway*

6 *Future Application*

BIBLE VERSE MAPPING

1 *The Verse*

Date : ___/___/___

2 *Translations of the verse*

3 *Keywords and definitions*

4 *Context of Verse*

Surrounding verses :

Who :

What :

Where :

When :

5 *Main Takeaway*

6 *Future Application*

BIBLE VERSE MAPPING

1 *The Verse*

Date : ___ / ___ / ___

2 *Translations of the verse*

3 *Keywords and definitions*

4 *Context of Verse*

Surrounding verses :

Who :   What :

Where :   When :

5 *Main Takeaway*

6 *Future Application*

BIBLE VERSE MAPPING

1 *The Verse*

2 *Translations of the verse*

3 *Keywords and definitions*

4 *Context of Verse*

Surrounding verses :

Who :   What :

Where :   When :

5 *Main Takeaway*

6 *Future Application*

BIBLE VERSE MAPPING

1 *The Verse*

Date : ___ / ___ / ___

2 *Translations of the verse*

3 *Keywords and definitions*

4 *Context of Verse*

Surrounding verses :

Who :

What :

Where :

When :

5 *Main Takeaway*

6 *Future Application*

BIBLE VERSE MAPPING

1 *The Verse*

Date : ___/___/___

2 *Translations of the verse*

3 *Keywords and definitions*

4 *Context of Verse*

Surrounding verses :

Who :

What :

Where :

When :

5 *Main Takeaway*

6 *Future Application*

BIBLE VERSE MAPPING

1 The Verse

Date : ___/___/___

2 Translations of the verse

3 Keywords and definitions

4 Context of Verse

Surrounding verses :

Who :

What :

Where :

When :

5 Main Takeaway

6 Future Application

BIBLE VERSE MAPPING

1 *The Verse*

Date : ___ / ___ / ___

2 *Translations of the verse*

3 *Keywords and definitions*

4 *Context of Verse*

Surrounding verses :

Who :

What :

Where :

When :

5 *Main Takeaway*

6 *Future Application*

BIBLE VERSE MAPPING

1 *The Verse*   *Date :* ___ / ___ / ___

2 *Translations of the verse*   **3** *Keywords and definitions*

4 *Context of Verse*

Surrounding verses :

Who :   *What :*

Where :   *When :*

5 *Main Takeaway*   **6** *Future Application*

BIBLE VERSE MAPPING

1 *The Verse*

Date : ___ / ___ / ___

2 *Translations of the verse*

3 *Keywords and definitions*

4 *Context of Verse*

Surrounding verses :

Who :

What :

Where :

When :

5 *Main Takeaway*

6 *Future Application*

BIBLE VERSE MAPPING

1 *The Verse*

Date : ___ / ___ / ___

2 *Translations of the verse*

3 *Keywords and definitions*

4 *Context of Verse*

Surrounding verses :

Who :

What :

Where :

When :

5 *Main Takeaway*

6 *Future Application*

BIBLE VERSE MAPPING

1 *The Verse*

Date : ___/___/___

2 *Translations of the verse*

3 *Keywords and definitions*

4 *Context of Verse*

Surrounding verses :

Who :

What :

Where :

When :

5 *Main Takeaway*

6 *Future Application*

BIBLE VERSE MAPPING

1 *The Verse*

Date : ___/ ___/ ___

2 *Translations of the verse*

3 *Keywords and definitions*

4 *Context of Verse*

Surrounding verses :

Who :

What :

Where :

When :

5 *Main Takeaway*

6 *Future Application*

BIBLE VERSE MAPPING

1 *The Verse*

Date : ___ / ___ / ___

2 *Translations of the verse*

3 *Keywords and definitions*

4 *Context of Verse*

Surrounding verses :

Who :   What :

Where :   When :

5 *Main Takeaway*

6 *Future Application*

BIBLE VERSE MAPPING

1 *The Verse*

Date : ___ / ___ / ___

2 *Translations of the verse*

3 *Keywords and definitions*

4 *Context of Verse*

Surrounding verses :

Who :

What :

Where :

When :

5 *Main Takeaway*

6 *Future Application*

BIBLE VERSE MAPPING

1 *The Verse*

Date : ___ / ___ / ___

2 *Translations of the verse*

3 *Keywords and definitions*

4 *Context of Verse*

Surrounding verses :

Who :

What :

Where :

When :

5 *Main Takeaway*

6 *Future Application*

BIBLE VERSE MAPPING

1 *The Verse*

Date : ___ / ___ / ___

2 *Translations of the verse*

3 *Keywords and definitions*

4 *Context of Verse*

Surrounding verses :

Who :   What :

Where :   When :

5 *Main Takeaway*

6 *Future Application*

BIBLE VERSE MAPPING

1 *The Verse*

Date : ___ / ___ / ___

2 *Translations of the verse*

3 *Keywords and definitions*

4 *Context of Verse*

Surrounding verses :

Who :

What :

Where :

When :

5 *Main Takeaway*

6 *Future Application*

BIBLE VERSE MAPPING

1 *The Verse*

Date : ___/ ___/ ___

2 *Translations of the verse*

3 *Keywords and definitions*

4 *Context of Verse*

Surrounding verses :

Who :

What :

Where :

When :

5 *Main Takeaway*

6 *Future Application*

BIBLE VERSE MAPPING

1 *The Verse*   *Date* : ___/___/___

2 *Translations of the verse*   **3** *Keywords and definitions*

4 *Context of Verse*

Surrounding verses :

Who :   *What* :

Where :   *When* :

5 *Main Takeaway*   **6** *Future Application*

BIBLE VERSE MAPPING

1 *The Verse*

Date : ___ / ___ / ___

2 *Translations of the verse*

3 *Keywords and definitions*

4 *Context of Verse*

Surrounding verses :

Who :

What :

Where :

When :

5 *Main Takeaway*

6 *Future Application*

BIBLE VERSE MAPPING

1 *The Verse*

Date : ___/___/___

2 *Translations of the verse*

3 *Keywords and definitions*

4 *Context of Verse*

Surrounding verses :

Who :

What :

Where :

When :

5 *Main Takeaway*

6 *Future Application*

BIBLE VERSE MAPPING

1 *The Verse*

Date : ___/___/___

2 *Translations of the verse*

3 *Keywords and definitions*

4 *Context of Verse*

Surrounding verses :

Who :

What :

Where :

When :

5 *Main Takeaway*

6 *Future Application*

BIBLE VERSE MAPPING

1 *The Verse*   *Date : ___ / ___ / ___*

2 *Translations of the verse*   **3** *Keywords and definitions*

4 *Context of Verse*

Surrounding verses :

Who :   *What :*

Where :   *When :*

5 *Main Takeaway*   **6** *Future Application*

BIBLE VERSE MAPPING

1 *The Verse*

Date : ___/___/___

2 *Translations of the verse*

3 *Keywords and definitions*

4 *Context of Verse*

Surrounding verses :

Who :

What :

Where :

When :

5 *Main Takeaway*

6 *Future Application*

BIBLE VERSE MAPPING

1 *The Verse*　　　　　　　　　　Date : ___ / ___ / ___

2 *Translations of the verse*　　　　**3** *Keywords and definitions*

4 *Context of Verse*

Surrounding verses :

Who :　　　　　　　　　　　What :

Where :　　　　　　　　　　When :

5 *Main Takeaway*　　　　　　　**6** *Future Application*

BIBLE VERSE MAPPING

1 *The Verse*

2 *Translations of the verse*

3 *Keywords and definitions*

4 *Context of Verse*

Surrounding verses :

Who :

What :

Where :

When :

5 *Main Takeaway*

6 *Future Application*

BIBLE VERSE MAPPING

1 *The Verse*

Date : ___/___/___

2 *Translations of the verse*

3 *Keywords and definitions*

4 *Context of Verse*

Surrounding verses :

Who :

What :

Where :

When :

5 *Main Takeaway*

6 *Future Application*

BIBLE VERSE MAPPING

1 *The Verse*   *Date : ___/ ___/ ___*

2 *Translations of the verse*   **3** *Keywords and definitions*

4 *Context of Verse*

Surrounding verses :

Who :   What :

Where :   When :

5 *Main Takeaway*   **6** *Future Application*

BIBLE VERSE MAPPING

1 *The Verse*

Date : ___ / ___ / ___

2 *Translations of the verse*

3 *Keywords and definitions*

4 *Context of Verse*

Surrounding verses :

Who :

What :

Where :

When :

5 *Main Takeaway*

6 *Future Application*

BIBLE VERSE MAPPING

1 *The Verse*

Date : ___ / ___ / ___

2 *Translations of the verse*

3 *Keywords and definitions*

4 *Context of Verse*

Surrounding verses :

Who :

What :

Where :

When :

5 *Main Takeaway*

6 *Future Application*

BIBLE VERSE MAPPING

1 The Verse

Date : ___ / ___ / ___

2 Translations of the verse

3 Keywords and definitions

4 Context of Verse

Surrounding verses :

Who :

What :

Where :

When :

5 Main Takeaway

6 Future Application

BIBLE VERSE MAPPING

1 *The Verse*

Date : ___/___/___

2 *Translations of the verse*

3 *Keywords and definitions*

4 *Context of Verse*

Surrounding verses :

Who :

What :

Where :

When :

5 *Main Takeaway*

6 *Future Application*

BIBLE VERSE MAPPING

1 *The Verse*

Date : ___ / ___ / ___

2 *Translations of the verse*

3 *Keywords and definitions*

4 *Context of Verse*

Surrounding verses :

Who :

What :

Where :

When :

5 *Main Takeaway*

6 *Future Application*

BIBLE VERSE MAPPING

1 *The Verse*

Date : ___ / ___ / ___

2 *Translations of the verse*

3 *Keywords and definitions*

4 *Context of Verse*

Surrounding verses :

Who :

What :

Where :

When :

5 *Main Takeaway*

6 *Future Application*

BIBLE VERSE MAPPING

1 *The Verse*

Date : ___ / ___ / ___

2 *Translations of the verse*

3 *Keywords and definitions*

4 *Context of Verse*

Surrounding verses :

Who :

What :

Where :

When :

5 *Main Takeaway*

6 *Future Application*

BIBLE VERSE MAPPING

1 *The Verse*

Date : ___/ ___/ ___

2 *Translations of the verse*

3 *Keywords and definitions*

4 *Context of Verse*

Surrounding verses :

Who :

What :

Where :

When :

5 *Main Takeaway*

6 *Future Application*

BIBLE VERSE MAPPING

1 *The Verse*

Date : ___/___/___

2 *Translations of the verse*

3 *Keywords and definitions*

4 *Context of Verse*

Surrounding verses :

Who :

What :

Where :

When :

5 *Main Takeaway*

6 *Future Application*

BIBLE VERSE MAPPING

1 *The Verse*

Date : ___ / ___ / ___

2 *Translations of the verse*

3 *Keywords and definitions*

4 *Context of Verse*

Surrounding verses :

Who :

What :

Where :

When :

5 *Main Takeaway*

6 *Future Application*

BIBLE VERSE MAPPING

1 *The Verse*   *Date :* ___/ ___/ ___

2 *Translations of the verse*   **3** *Keywords and definitions*

4 *Context of Verse*

Surrounding verses :

Who :   *What :*

Where :   *When :*

5 *Main Takeaway*   **6** *Future Application*

BIBLE VERSE MAPPING

1 *The Verse*

Date : ___/___/___

2 *Translations of the verse*

3 *Keywords and definitions*

4 *Context of Verse*

Surrounding verses :

Who :

What :

Where :

When :

5 *Main Takeaway*

6 *Future Application*

BIBLE VERSE MAPPING

1 *The Verse*

Date : ___/___/___

2 *Translations of the verse*

3 *Keywords and definitions*

4 *Context of Verse*

Surrounding verses :

Who :

What :

Where :

When :

5 *Main Takeaway*

6 *Future Application*

BIBLE VERSE MAPPING

1 *The Verse*

Date : ___ / ___ / ___

2 *Translations of the verse*

3 *Keywords and definitions*

4 *Context of Verse*

Surrounding verses :

Who :

What :

Where :

When :

5 *Main Takeaway*

6 *Future Application*

BIBLE VERSE MAPPING

1 *The Verse*

Date : ___/___/___

2 *Translations of the verse*

3 *Keywords and definitions*

4 *Context of Verse*

Surrounding verses :

Who :

What :

Where :

When :

5 *Main Takeaway*

6 *Future Application*

BIBLE VERSE MAPPING

1 *The Verse*

Date : ___/___/___

2 *Translations of the verse*

3 *Keywords and definitions*

4 *Context of Verse*

Surrounding verses :

Who :   What :

Where :   When :

5 *Main Takeaway*

6 *Future Application*

BIBLE VERSE MAPPING

1 *The Verse*

Date : ___ / ___ / ___

2 *Translations of the verse*

3 *Keywords and definitions*

4 *Context of Verse*

Surrounding verses :

Who :

What :

Where :

When :

5 *Main Takeaway*

6 *Future Application*

BIBLE VERSE MAPPING

1 *The Verse*

Date : ___ / ___ / ___

2 *Translations of the verse*

3 *Keywords and definitions*

4 *Context of Verse*

Surrounding verses :

Who :

What :

Where :

When :

5 *Main Takeaway*

6 *Future Application*

BIBLE VERSE MAPPING

1 *The Verse*

Date : ___ / ___ / ___

2 *Translations of the verse*

3 *Keywords and definitions*

4 *Context of Verse*

Surrounding verses :

Who :

What :

Where :

When :

5 *Main Takeaway*

6 *Future Application*

BIBLE VERSE MAPPING

1 *The Verse*

Date : ___/___/___

2 *Translations of the verse*

3 *Keywords and definitions*

4 *Context of Verse*

Surrounding verses :

Who :

What :

Where :

When :

5 *Main Takeaway*

6 *Future Application*

BIBLE VERSE MAPPING

1 *The Verse*

Date : ___ / ___ / ___

2 *Translations of the verse*

3 *Keywords and definitions*

4 *Context of Verse*

Surrounding verses :

Who :

What :

Where :

When :

5 *Main Takeaway*

6 *Future Application*

BIBLE VERSE MAPPING

1 *The Verse*

Date : ___ / ___ / ___

2 *Translations of the verse*

3 *Keywords and definitions*

4 *Context of Verse*

Surrounding verses :

Who :

What :

Where :

When :

5 *Main Takeaway*

6 *Future Application*

BIBLE VERSE MAPPING

1 *The Verse*   *Date* : ___/ ___/ ___

2 *Translations of the verse*   **3** *Keywords and definitions*

4 *Context of Verse*

Surrounding verses :

Who :   What :

Where :   When :

5 *Main Takeaway*   **6** *Future Application*

BIBLE VERSE MAPPING

1 *The Verse*

Date : ___/ ___/ ___

2 *Translations of the verse*

3 *Keywords and definitions*

4 *Context of Verse*

Surrounding verses :

Who :

What :

Where :

When :

5 *Main Takeaway*

6 *Future Application*

BIBLE VERSE MAPPING

1 *The Verse*

Date : ___/___/___

2 *Translations of the verse*

3 *Keywords and definitions*

4 *Context of Verse*

Surrounding verses :

Who :

What :

Where :

When :

5 *Main Takeaway*

6 *Future Application*

BIBLE VERSE MAPPING

1 *The Verse*

Date : ___/___/___

2 *Translations of the verse*

3 *Keywords and definitions*

4 *Context of Verse*

Surrounding verses :

Who :

What :

Where :

When :

5 *Main Takeaway*

6 *Future Application*

BIBLE VERSE MAPPING

1 *The Verse*

Date : ___ / ___ / ___

2 *Translations of the verse*

3 *Keywords and definitions*

4 *Context of Verse*

Surrounding verses :

Who :   What :

Where :   When :

5 *Main Takeaway*

6 *Future Application*

BIBLE VERSE MAPPING

1 *The Verse*

Date : ___/ ___/ ___

2 *Translations of the verse*

3 *Keywords and definitions*

4 *Context of Verse*

Surrounding verses :

Who :

What :

Where :

When :

5 *Main Takeaway*

6 *Future Application*

BIBLE VERSE MAPPING

1 The Verse

Date : ___/___/___

2 Translations of the verse

3 Keywords and definitions

4 Context of Verse

Surrounding verses :

Who :

What :

Where :

When :

5 Main Takeaway

6 Future Application

BIBLE VERSE MAPPING

1 *The Verse*

Date : ___ / ___ / ___

2 *Translations of the verse*

3 *Keywords and definitions*

4 *Context of Verse*

Surrounding verses :

Who :

What :

Where :

When :

5 *Main Takeaway*

6 *Future Application*

BIBLE VERSE MAPPING

1 The Verse

Date : ___/___/___

2 Translations of the verse

3 Keywords and definitions

4 Context of Verse

Surrounding verses :

Who :

Where :

What :

When :

5 Main Takeaway

6 Future Application

BIBLE VERSE MAPPING

1 *The Verse*

Date : ___/ ___/ ___

2 *Translations of the verse*

3 *Keywords and definitions*

4 *Context of Verse*

Surrounding verses :

Who :

What :

Where :

When :

5 *Main Takeaway*

6 *Future Application*

BIBLE VERSE MAPPING

1 *The Verse*

Date : ___ / ___ / ___

2 *Translations of the verse*

3 *Keywords and definitions*

4 *Context of Verse*

Surrounding verses :

Who :

What :

Where :

When :

5 *Main Takeaway*

6 *Future Application*

BIBLE VERSE MAPPING

1 *The Verse*

Date : ___/___/___

2 *Translations of the verse*

3 *Keywords and definitions*

4 *Context of Verse*

Surrounding verses :

Who :

What :

Where :

When :

5 *Main Takeaway*

6 *Future Application*

BIBLE VERSE MAPPING

1 *The Verse*

Date : ___/___/___

2 *Translations of the verse*

3 *Keywords and definitions*

4 *Context of Verse*

Surrounding verses :

Who :

What :

Where :

When :

5 *Main Takeaway*

6 *Future Application*

BIBLE VERSE MAPPING

1 *The Verse*

Date : ___/___/___

2 *Translations of the verse*

3 *Keywords and definitions*

4 *Context of Verse*

Surrounding verses :

Who :

What :

Where :

When :

5 *Main Takeaway*

6 *Future Application*

BIBLE VERSE MAPPING

1 *The Verse*

Date : ___ / ___ / ___

2 *Translations of the verse*

3 *Keywords and definitions*

4 *Context of Verse*

Surrounding verses :

Who :

What :

Where :

When :

5 *Main Takeaway*

6 *Future Application*

BIBLE VERSE MAPPING

1 *The Verse*

Date : ___/___/___

2 *Translations of the verse*

3 *Keywords and definitions*

4 *Context of Verse*

Surrounding verses :

Who :

What :

Where :

When :

5 *Main Takeaway*

6 *Future Application*

Made in the USA
Las Vegas, NV
13 February 2024